A WHISPERING

Geoffrey Heptonstall

ISBN: 978-81-19228-18-8

First Edition: 2023
Rs. 200/-

Cyberwit.net
HIG 45 Kaushambi Kunj, Kalindipuram
Allahabad - 211011 (U.P.) India
http://www.cyberwit.net
Tel: +(91) 9415091004
E-mail: info@cyberwit.net

Printed at Vcore.

Some of these poems first appeared in *Adirondack Review*, *Blank Pages, Caught in the Net*, *Dead Ink*, *English, The Flying Dodo*, *Ink Sweat and Tears*, *International Literary Quarterly*, *Jasper's Folly*, *London Grip*, *London Progressive Journal, Message in a Bottle*, *New Linear Perspectives*, *Nine Muses*, *Pangolin Review*, *The Pen*, *Penwood Review, The Poet*, *Poetry Monthly*, *The Poetry Shed*, *Poetry Super Highway*, *Poetry Village*, *The Recusant*, *Turbulence* and *Visual Verse*

The Tree that Stood in the Field appeared in *The Highland Park Poetry Anthology* (2020)

To Another Day appeared in the anthology *Our Changing Earth* (2023)

Belated thanks to the Cambridge Poetry Café.

My love always to my wife Debbie for her boundless inspiration, acute intellect and selfless devotion.

Contents

1. DOWN TO EARTH

Explorations in the Natural World

A WORLD TOO WIDE

On learning how the world was made
in dreams of human love revealed
when spring water flows through empty streets,
and children's dreams fall to earth.
On high vantage the lover sees all
that he adores withdraw
as the sea returns to the shore
like lightning in the summer heat.
Wild horses ride across the bay.
What part can the heart play
in the sound of a single note
in an empty auditorium?
Everything alert seeks shelter.
Our hopes anticipate change.

AN OPENING FLOWER

In demeanour frivolous.
The strategy was surely natural,
no more acquiescence to a myth
but an accomplished style displayed,
articulating the hour that comes,
a history of artifice,
exemplary, elegiac and eloquent
when many things are beginning
with a harvest of gilded whispers.

The future is many speculations
that move with the change of time
never to be entirely abandoned.
But *Now* is the endless prospect,
a charcoal sketch of perceptions,
a season's sour-sweet longing
available to the spirited and aware
in their worldly innocence
why the contours remain shaded.

The young have eyes for their moon world
where love above all is possible
with new growth rising after the storm,
immediate and miraculously alive
to the taste of the moment's intention.
Trees in the breeze sway outside the window.
Blossom showers the glass dampened by rain
Demurely she moves through the garden,
she who defines the opening flower.

EARTH IS OURS

A hand goes down to fecund ground
reaching the heart found in the depths,
those whispers of their grace within.
Earth is ours by invitation.
Nothing is given without cause.
When shutters are open to the morning
sun burns the dew on summer dream lawns.
Every blade a blessing from the green world
until to the eye all is perfection
with angels and swans passing by,
finding their way to another life.
The signs are in the air,
occasionally it is a cloud,
more often the shape of light
painting the dawn and the dusk
and every hour that forms the day.
A hand may reach to touch the sky,
only to find heaven's laughter echoing.

A HART'S DEATH

In spring the untended stems
sway in their wayward reach.
There is a sky darkening,
the shadow of cloud on water.
These flowers are for the sun,
as the forest is for the fugitive.

The sacrifice of self by fear
demands a steady hand
in the hunting of the wild,
all energy dispersed in flight.
The hunting hounds can follow
to the end of earth,
saltwater shingle strand
where the trail runs cold.
And there the solitude cries
sequestered from the world.

Leaping from the page,
the death seems natural
when the hunting book opens.

A creature of the dream
seeks shade in open spaces.
And there the hart's cries
are heard in the mansion sound,
mausoleum of marble,

cool in an unfurnished mind.
And here the hart
capable of being broken,
Insistent echoes are open.

THE TREE THAT STOOD IN THE FIELD

The season made no difference:
in heat haze, mist or cloudiness
the tree that stood in the field was stark.
Its texture had the look of charcoal.
There were no leaves to green the year.

Soundless, it issued an invitation
to stare at the spectral agony
torn out of nature,
a life taken, by lightning struck.

Like a rare bird, it hovered
on the parish bounds,
evading loyalties.
It knew its otherness
to be the way of survival.
Certain of one thing only,
the fear we have of dying.

And to a child the strange scene
compelled our dark imaginings:
by moonlight it moved, of course,
dancing to the midnight music.

Something could be heard,
a rumour whispered as we watched.
touching the tree turned you to stone.
No-one was tempted to try.
This was where the wild men roamed.

Their shadows passed the windows of sleep.
'It's only the swaying of trees.'

The wind that moved the branches
brought the storms that changed our world.
A rain of fire had burnt the soul.

AN ISLAND SUMMER

Then is the absence of everything,
having flown out of history.
There is danger within sight.
The first act is always the same.
The scene has been played many times:
ragged children embody innocence
until reality overtakes them.
The melody is eloquent, of course,
in a cloudless midsummer sky.

Now let us consider how wars begin
before the souring of the springs
and the sound of devils' tongues
heard in the ruins of what was once
with agonized eyes staring.

Everything is named by the gods.
We wonder is there another world
named now for another god
from the first day of creation?
A question as old as Eden.
Answers are seen in the sky,
leaving only an echo in the air.

This island has many seasons.
Life has to be learned again
The summer before had been cold.
There was a migration southward
into uncertainty and fear

as the moment of departure came.
Rumours of a violent scattering
floated downstream in the fall.

Fearing the sun will not rise again,
barefoot in the snow they run
from the sound of horsemen
who have rode the ocean waves
always flowing from infinity.

The tracks in the snow are easily seen
for the horsemen to follow at dawn
with the death they have become.
They day that came had been foretold.
The earth has changed rotation.
Stars have fallen in showers
of fire that burn the flesh
from the bones of innocence,
a storm to breach the harbour wall,
a withering of the vine before harvest,
a candle burning down the house,
a singing voice stilled in mid-song.
White sails on the horizon came,
misted in their spectral pallor.
Dogs began their incessant barking
beneath the shadow of bird flight.
The trees of the forest stared starkly
when the ships pass by the rocks.
Some devil saw them to shore.

THE ESTUARY STATION

Dreaming travellers wait for the city,
imagining horizons could end
imprisoned experience
beneath clear skies
and shining water
from distant hills.

The rail holds to land precariously
as almost-sea encroaches.
Trains sail the peninsula.
Some seem Baltic-bound.
Others may never find their way
when tidal currents must flow their course.

This unknown nowhere,
chilled by its vastness,
is to someone home,
her haven land
where endless journeys
reach a welcome paragon.

A TRAIL OF INNOCENCE

The sure necessity of life
according to the mind of nature
is the way the earth moves.
There are patterns of a natural plan
even with uncertain changes
in another season of the cycle
with a memory of the days.

The ash tree leaves, dry on the fingers,
are always the first to fall.
They lie on September soil, waiting.
October winds will float them away.
On coastal waters the waders rise
as the last of daylight fades.
They are tempted by the moon.

On the vantage hill at sunrise
an unseen something moves close by.
Slight sounds betray a watchful eye.
on the dawn walker's lonely trail.
Human innocence is a rare sight.
Danger never seems far from view.
This forage, this flight may be the last.

A WINTER'S SIGHT

Across the bay the city rises.
Wintering on the horizon line
is all the ocean finds of life,
though the mood changes by the hour.

How may the winter wake
when mist is no metaphor
in an invisible world?
All we can hear is unconnected,
so many misunderstandings,
like a bride at a funeral.
No-one can believe what is there.

On a bridge we have yet to cross
the end is stumbling innocence
that searches for a crack in the ice.
We want to watch the winter flow
down to the opening sea.
So many have gone in the meantime
while others are planning a return.

The intention is to enlighten
all the items of natural interest,
a suggestion of vague certainties.
They may be heard in unsheltered air
until all that falls are unspoken words.
They dance in graceful determination.
Something escapes from the fading light
when snow descends in slow congress

with the rhythm of a day's reflection,
words that hope to speak well of things.
Sounds lap against the land's incline,
a conversation never ending.
Every voyage a rough translation,
seeking a useful measure of space.

Tick, tick, tick of the clockmaker's craft.
The need of the hour is to watch
and record the incoming flow.
The confession is now complete.

2. ON SACRED GROUND

Considerations of Faith and Mystery

THE WILD MEN

The dust blows from the sandstone mounds,
falling as rumours in the summer haze.
The intimacy of the village senses
something in the almost urban
where the spirit of wilderness remains
unearthed in ancient bones.
History is revealed as real and uncertain.
There is strong ground here for believing
a presence in the nature of the land.
Observations for rational eyes
pale and fade in the shadow of the strangers
mute and naked with animal innocence.
The wild men are seen to wander
in ways once familiar, now unknown.

HOPE STREET

Yet stranger than we suppose,
the stars shine on the night sea.
Somewhere in the city
they shiver in the shadow of God.
See those mendicant men,
alert as attendant lords,
waiting for the world to turn.
At six o'clock sounds the hour
for the solitary optimist
who walks the moon in search of her.

Beneath her grace lies unseen
the indefinite, unknown her.
It compels the better part of him
to dream and to wake in one breath.
His mouth is open for that tongue
to taste the air of her.
He watches the trees dancing.
They make quadrilles at sunset before the city
assures the fearful children
taking the road homeward.

This moment life begins to be lived in one day.
It is all we can see moving slowly in the night sky.

STEPPING STONES

In the crumbling walls a fissure
where fingers may reach into history.
An occasional issue of fragments
born of myth that is truth's armature
entombed for an eternity
that can never endure.
The walls have a way of speaking
when there is no-one to overhear,
except the wind that carries an echo
often mistaken for the clip-clip of rain.
History faces the elemental force
that works its way into being.

An archipelago of the fallen,
stonework no longer withstanding
the natural course of change
until the transformation carves its name.
What are such works but stepping stones
trodden lightly as the sleepers stir?
One testimony at a time
written in the dust as the walls give way
At sunrise the words will scatter
all the fragile secrets long withheld,
attending on the moment of uncovering.
In history the time is always now.

A WHISPERING

The Duchess, she has eluded me,
and I have yet to see her.
Once we sailed from Amalfi
into the Odyssean waters
as if to hear an unearthly song.
The surface was a foreboding calm,
like the soundless dark of a new moon.
Something cold was close at hand,
as sharp as a diamond tear.

No elaboration required.
Curiosity is eager to please
when acceptance must answer
in a private performance
of indelicate questioning
for a public rehearsal
that makes nonsense of the query.
Chance is the only choice
for the sake of the union.

In the waters of Byzantium
Medusa presides over the springs.
She is a hidden, harmless image
of malevolence sequestered.
Wisdom is the patron saint
of the city that sails many oceans.
The faithful invite the infidel
to pray for the peace of the world.
And someone speaks of Jerusalem.

Of course you have heard the name
where nothing remains unknown
in the state of self-discovery.
Admitting the truth is so much
more than can be denied
in every urgent resolution.
An understanding must be clear,
a stage set for a solitary quest.
Truth is inclined to say yes.

There are nights when the world is open.
I find a note written with grace,
there to be discovered in time
read amid rumours of lasting change.
The lines were Webster's, unfamiliar
and dark as a Jacobean mind.
It was she herself speaking
in defiance of untimely death:
'*So that I were out of your whispering.*'

JERUSALEM

The sound of an opening door:
they were speaking of Jerusalem,
a word that made a city
a sacred space for all believers.
There our hearts may find heaven
even at first sight of its promise,
the celestial shimmering
where many faiths gather as one.
They search for the mystery of life,
the harmony that becomes a holy name.
We name it as Jerusalem.
May it be the city of peace
for the sake of everywhere
within the walls embracing the world.

CHAMBER MUSIC

Where once was Jericho falling
to the music of one mind
the stones have risen unseen.
There is no way of finding
the words that never fade
when written in the air.
None dare ask of anyone
the answer to the question
'Who walks into this world?'

How the mind may leap
higher than a hand can reach.
There is no way of knowing
all that is passing unaware
of how it may appear to be
the sound heard only in silence
from the far side of the universe
where the walls have an ending.

Every thought an echo
of a voice once heard.
The speaker is unknown.

THE JOURNEY OF THE MAGI

The wishes of children escape
the grasp of chilled fingers
tracing the tracks in the snow.
Hopes like these float across the world
on a clear, star-scattered night.
One light especially shines
in the time of the year's ending.
What begins in moonlight becomes
more than can be imagined
when delighted eyes open,
like the gates of an unknown future
slowly revealing our reason for being.

MEMENTO MORI

Sometimes there is music
in the well-tended churchyard.
Victorians below stir in their sleep.
Some only knew childhood,
then they were no more.
But not for ever now.

We find an inventory of disease:
typhus, cholera, consumption.
Or there was childbirth…

The pattern of stars we see
are theirs also. So, too,
the seasonal shifts of earth
we share with them.

History is waxwork,
but on this common ground
are lives of many kinds,
falling as water on stone
where something thoughtful is written:

And in the Beginning
there was Everything

THE RETURN

The footprints were visible
when he promised to return.
He was there and elsewhere
in the rain, in the dust,
in the wind, in the heat.
In truth he was everywhere
half-heard in the crowd,
so like the words he offered.
A shadow that spoke
from a tongue they could see
there at the table, speaking.
No more than a flame in the fire,
serene and unworldly
now in his expression.
The wound no longer bled,
but open still and yet to heal.
There was no pain.

OF ALL KNOWING

And there will be a time
where beginnings have endings
for the sun has risen long ago
or so it seems in memory.
The air is mild for the season.

Measuring eternity, another hour passes.
Full leafing trees stand laden
with knowledge on a bowing branch,
an eyebrow's arc of surprise.
on seeing the scene again.

A high flow of tides makes an island world
but life intervenes if the promise survives.
She is born into light and shadow
an ocean of the mind where lives marooned
pass years of time reaching back beyond
dust falling from stone, gathering into stars,
a myth made real by nature that leads from source,
its water encompassing what is seen of the world.
On this the trees determine:
They have not seen all they can,
and so are moving all the way
to eternity, source of all knowing
how the good fruit falls.

3. LIVING IN THE WORLD

Confronting the Realities of Life

LONDON

She feeds the swans on the waters,
chases wild geese wherever they fly,
knows the name of every stranger
she greets on her long way home.

In dark places incivility insists
from faces Goya could have painted:
the stare of the skeletal penitent,
the snarl of the angry thief.
Souls waiting for oblivion's edge.

She knows the streets of London
are paved with gilded good intentions.
She walks in the haze of her hunger.
The darker places are hers alone.
Life is lived without a moon.

Midnight finds her usual shelter,
and so she sleeps in Neverland
until at first light and cold she rises
as if a fortune were hers.

Today she will not die.

A LONDON WALK, 1665

It was fire that brought deliverance,
considered a strange mercy,
or by some a further punishment,
its presence taken as a curse
touching the flesh before it decays.
To walk among the spirits of the city
gave temperance to those in strife,
so near a view of the end of life.
Go down, damned, to a visible hell.

Of cause unknown contagion came
with dreams of a universal end.
Some saw apparitions in sunlight,
then the sight of a blazing star.
So many spoke in a delirium.
Others were given to wild wandering.
'Reason brings order, but few pay heed....
These things terrified the people.'
Defoe, of course, imagined it well.

WHAT TEMPTATION SAYS

Opening a cutting claw,
and all is well when it is not.
The light is only incidental.
Shadows of perfection pass.
The bird of fortune swoops
on wings that leave their maker's mark.
So says temptation, beckoning
the worm that weaves its thread
in the silken surface of sky.
When it goes there is no more
in tempting law of transparency,
instinctive and aware.
An ear to hear the sound beneath her
is soon to be the moth that flies
where the caterpillar crawls.
The facts of love and death
may be found in delicate cocoons
not yet expressed in words.
There are none, temptation says.

RECREATION GROUND

The tall ships sail past all conjecture.
Soon they shall be horizon
and then no more.
As for the clouds,
we shall pass through them
when at last we make our leap.

By the nettled grass with brambles
an awkward child – still and smiling –
is looking upward,
arms outstretched.
Somewhere in him is a memory
of the games he plays with the moon.

We fly with balloons in the park
a blind man sells from the shade.
Perfect days are rare, he says.
But he will not stand in the sun.
His world is vague, almost shapeless.
Only the closest things exist.

Wishing him well from the sky,
we dream in sunlight of summer things.
And for sure the monstrous mouth opens
to devour all it sees of innocence.

AN EDUCATION IN POVERTY

As plain as a simple source,
a matter of unknown lives
sharp and clean, a grinding stone
clearing the dust when there is work.
Hunger always rises in the mind,
a lesson learned, unheard and unsung.
An afterlife is beyond all chosen words
hurrying to the fields at dawn.
From empty streets the usual lesson
is forever learned by heart.

THE ENDLESS ROOM

There are no secrets to be found
beyond the endless room.
It was always implied
in every indiscretion of voices
the walls were heard to echo,
revealing all that could happen again
reaching out to infinity,
saying what all eyes could see
to be a sound strategy.

So readily she saw the room
softly lit and quietly measured,
the sign on the door read well,
saying what all eyes could see
when she entered the room
for the sake of becoming.
A life passes from the first moment.
Earth a fragile child,
a masterpiece in the mind's eye,
lives the moment of Creation.

From one life to another
all is spoken into being.
Things so familiar fade
into a trail of whispers.
The word is the world
as distant stars approach, like souls,
once lost, now homeward bound.
The moment came by chance,

an experience of itself
following the light across the room
until all was radiance,

The future is perfect.

TO ANOTHER DAY

Roof beams rise until time begins.
The walls of the city shimmer.
A spectre walks in the sun,
What almost touched heaven falls.
The sound stirs the mind of reason,
and opening eyes ask why.
Somewhere a distant star falls
beyond here and before now.
almost close to the heart.

The sky remains as pale as bones.
No shade to be found from the sun,
nor shelter from the winter wind
when fires burn what was to have been.
Another day's familiar dawn,
say the birds returning
to their care of the scene
the dogs have torn from life
in the silent city streets.

When the day cools they begin
their roaming of a darker place.
They wait for the taste of midnight.
They will not run until they hear
a bell intones the midnight hour.
What was there will be again
because the world is round.
That is the shape about to be.
No-one guards the future now.

INDIGO CAFÉ, CAMBRIDGE

The ghosts of Cambridge walk
with the words that survive
the madness of governing minds.
A philosopher's silence speaks
of eloquent fears revealed.
The world is real enough
when the burning begins.

In the Indigo Café we hear
there is serious rumour
of summer falling into darkness
as easily as war declares
the uncertainty of things
in the shadow of the sun
eclipsed by civil strife.

Voices passing by confirm
what is written in the air:
history has given its warning.
The book of redemption closes
when we are a whisper away
from the shattering of glass
and the breaking of bones.

FRAGMENTS

The care that will repair them
may never be broken
within this handmade world.
In the earthenware hollow,
a resounding echo of ocean.
The fragments lie in the dust
where they fell in slow descent.

In time the line of cutting fades.
and skin may hide the bone again.
The wound must leave a scar
by a moment's misfortune.

The jar that held cool water
rests on the ledge with pride.

IN THE WORLD WE HAVE CREATED

The statue casts a shadow in the square.
The astronomer's eye makes calculations
of the hour of the day according to the sun.

His world turns with the spheres in harmony.
He has seen hoe stars have life,
and that their light may die.

The earth is not eternal.
God makes bounds to His creation.
He has troubled the astronomers mind.
Madonnas shall weep for him.
A pitiless inquisitor will smile.

But on this afternoon there is peace in the colonnades.
This man of learning savours his wine.
A beauty passes his window.
Her kindliness renders the scene gracious.
It could be called celestial.

Later he sees in the stars how there is no fear
that truth will ever die.

THE SHAPE OF REASON

Consider the shape of reason encircling the world.
A conclusion follows the line of argument
when everything begins making sense of itself.

The colonnades at evening are cool, shaded all day from the sun.
The tables are set for dinner as waiters in classic black and
white surround us. Live Jazz begins, resonating in the arcade
that leads to the street out there. Galileo once worked close by.
This square he will have known.
Walking in the shade at about this hour he imagines the unseen
side of the moon, gazing into the sky in time to see her full,
generous figure. Her face is a perpetual enigma, appearing
variously on the walls of churches, palaces and museums.

The room where the inquisitor sits is bare. Galileo will make
patterns of the cracks and plaster blemishes of the white walls.
The shape, he notes, is not quite circular. It is not perfect.
Something was amiss in the making of this from its ideal plan.
But geometry, he remembers, has no feeling. And yet…
The plough in the furrow
has the contours of motion
made to a purpose,
It is shaped by necessity
in moving the earth
as the world turns.

HARVEST

There was rain falling
when I came close.
And the sound of a forgotten song
from a vacant house
gently touched my face,
my hopes murmuring.

The air was appled.
Also the ground where they had fallen.
We found them at ease in the grass
with the taste of several temptations.

What happens here will be natural
to an autumnal appetite.
There is something to celebrate
with the occasional confession.
After the harvest comes the feasting.
After that, her tenderness.

WHAT SHALL WE DO NEXT SUMMER?

In the streets about the museum
you will have heard news of the future:
next year the world will turn on a new axis,
beginning in spring when the water's rise.
All the power fails where thoughts rebel
leaving lives sequestered
in abandoned corners.

Something unforeseen in vermilion, moves
carefully across the square.
There were hints in the history lesson
children were taught yesterday.
Such words are summer lightning.
Citizens sing when the storm passes.
Next summer shall see more rain falling.
It will not be the same kind of rain.
Its colours will change the world.
Next summer we shall find time.

A VICTORIAN RELIC

The bell tolled in the asylum.
All other sound was abandoned.
They knew what was happening.
They were as children are, and so treated.
Sin was said to be in their souls.
The only cure was punishment.
None dared look but to wonder
who would be another nameless voice?

Fear raged like fire in the silence,
its stench a discharge of despair
far into the depths of shame.
Frail humanity imprisoned in stone,
cold flesh felt the strength within the walls.
Fists might bleed with raw anger.
This place was designed for innocence
to be derided and destroyed.

4. HOMEWARD BOUND

Remembering Family

PRIMAVERA

The house they built became my parents' life.
Some trees grew and others fell
levelling the foundations
in ploughed clay and sand of marsh islet earth.
They found fragments,
neither memory nor myth,
but a history marked on discarded maps,
a settlement no-one has seen.

Capable hands had carved the stones.
Spires of gothic fingers
traced the indented detail to the master's taste.
Mannered, on high ground,
was evidence of grandeur
that had passed with the shifts of the river,
defining the boundaries of parish
and what an eye may possess.

The new house was never still.
The sense, the shadow, almost the sound,
would haunt our presumption.
It was not a place to be alone.
Now it is somewhere remembered.
Other children listen for our tread.

TENDING THE VINES

When shadows crossed the sunlit lawns
before the world was invented.
We suppose time has chosen
how a garden gate might close
with the ending of the scene.

Such frail memorials
to lives everlasting
we keep as curators
of imagined cadavers.
What I can remember
are things I never knew.

THE CENTURY OF SARAH BAXTER

Both eyes of hers resemble the moon.
Her skin in the dawn is marble.
The hair in the wind falls wildly.
Or so I imagine how she was,
remembering that was then.
Think of her as history.
I am there, walking through time
to meet her who was young,
close by the sapling apple tree
that was felled in its prime.

Hunched with age, she spoke in sepia:
yoked with pails, she was a milkmaid.
Her burden belies the pastoral romance.
Then there came her marriage,
one of life's obligations
arranged in layers, like an onion
ripening in the earth before harvest.
These rites are learned by heart,
beginning with a modest glance
before skirts swirl as she dances.

On the brow of the hill she might see
beyond the line the lives unborn.
They were to be her reason.
A haze of possibilities shimmers.
At her feet are the flowers that blaze.
Once there was a lovers' season.
Sarah survived trials and temptations

among the remnants of her dreams
scattered through the pasture land.
Gracefully homeward an old lady wanders.

ANOTHER SUMMER

From the dunes, like snow,
the sand is contoured,
with wild grass in fine hollows.
What we see is real,
invisible to the eye.
Hoof prints of horses
mark a trail on the shore.
Tomorrow we shall be riders.

Sea charts show the nature of the waters,
Steering a channel clear of the shallows,
we wake in the morning to see pale horizon.
Close by the masts rise with the light.
The ships sway at anchor,
motioning to sail with the tide.

FOR THE FROST

Then there is home, the certainty
of expected domestic phrases
praising the extension,
admiring what remains of the trees
cut away, like the children
who were here and are now
somewhere within the garden
of memory and perception.

Tomorrow we drive across miles of openness,
searching an interest among the hills,
a place we have known,
another sacred history
we are pleased to collect
as the fresh snow falls on clear ground,
is swept cleanly away
before the frost makes glass of the carapace.

In the returning time
I think of the frost
ripening as the day falls,
and we hurry westward
because it finally is winter,
The Advent journey complete
in a gathering of hunters
whom, scarlet and posed, we pass.

There is someone waiting in the frost,
a cousin, distant and close,

who, appearing, lightens
whatever was, out of time again
when we speak, spring-like,
even in the chill
until he follows in,
remembering with 'Of course.'

In the morning we see
there the evidence
where Magi passed this way,
or so we wonder,
that there may be wisdom
which is the other season,
witnessed in winter,
spoken for the frost.

ONE MORE FROST

In this final winter,
home to a vacant house
in mourning style,
with ice on the sale sign.
unlit, but heated
by neighbourly care,
still it is voiceless.

A card for Christmas,
fallen on the floor,
postmark from Pennsville:
a cousin of one or the other,,
who has yet to hear
the slow march of long men
sounding in the night.

Our neighbours we know
and the fields are familiar.
but I name my navigators
among the departed.
The distance taken –
measureless in miles –
is nothing against the dust.

WINTER DREAM

In his dream it is summer again.
Always in these scenes he is young.
The city is unfamiliar,
though he knows it to be his own.
Someone walks with him.
In the dream it is a friend.
(It was no-one he knew.)
At the crossroads he says goodbye,
having a letter to post
before the daylight fades.

Through the dusk light he goes home.
There is she waiting.
The door eagerly opens
at the sound of his approach.
A supper for two is laid,
with the good wine he brings,
and flowers almost in full bloom.
She raises her head, smiling.

Later they walk in the garden,
then move once more upward.
The sun rose on another world
where in the night snow fell,
softer than frost,
harder than rain.
It rests on the jasmine
and burdens the elder trees.
Winter drifts in bitter dawn.
All life is held against the north wind.
He wakes, friendless in the cold.
There are no letters to send.

5. WHISPERS

Thoughts of Fear, Admiration and Love

ANOTHER ENDLESS NIGHT

Another endless night
that reason can never fulfil,
waiting without expectation
for restless minds wandering.
The voyage began hopelessly.
Clouds dispersed in moonlight,
seeing the water flow by.
Travellers in the dream of history
may speak in many tongues.
They are the tales they tell
now they have seen
there is an unknown land.
They find no conclusion,
nor reason to be seeking
so elegant a vision of something,
another endless night.

ENCOUNTERING VERLAINE

Invisible the sun that sets on our schemes.
Considering the division of the city,
we find our way in the dark forest,
following a thread of gold toward the nightingale.

The scene is the same:
in these remains of memory
enslaved to a dream,
he remembers images familiar,
of origin always unknown.

The whisperings insist:
he hears an orphan's plea
in the pale monotony
of an autumnal aquarelle
soon to be ruined in the rain.

The ordeal has an ending:
in her presence he is wearing
a mask of velvet reverence
that in time will appear
the dreamer's natural face.

He is living the time:
A face resembling the Moon,
her tender serenity
in the celestial cabaret's
sequestering innocence.

TIME SONG

The music of living:
the ethereal sensation
is the song of happenstance
to sing something of itself
now in the incidental moment.

In time a caged bird will be free.
The syncopation is natural,
dancing down the winding stair,
a rhythm that alerts the heart
with every measured beat.

In search of elusive harmony
songs rise with the sun,
remembered through the dark hours
summoning the will to be heard
sometimes here, at other times there.

The sound surrounds us.

A VAUDEVILLE SPIRIT

What ghost am I in the glass
when all I leave is my name?
A life in limelight,
a death in the wings,
the world is mad in my mind.
This has been my inspiration.
A million farthings delight the crowd
that sees a painted goose of a man.
So they may sing of champagne,
though laughter soon ends as dust.
I catch the applause with my silk hat
held in hands that have shaken princes'.
A cat may look at a quean,
and I admire the eyes of a lady
when from the gods I fly down,
feather light and eager to please.
No audience is ever the same
as the one I remember.

(Dan Leno, 1860-1904, thrilled and amused audiences, and inspired many performers who followed him, especially of course Charlie Chaplin. Leno died young in an asylum. His autobiography, *Dan Leno Hys Boke*, is a masterpiece of comic writing.)

THEATRE OF THE ABSURD

We were speaking of Beckett,
of the lyrical anxiety,
in several suspicions,
emotions of many kinds,
sometimes named for pity.

And the lives of strangers
are a living memory,
a cry of the condemned
submerged in dark chambers.

We choose like executioners
what we cannot hear
even in the winter night.

THE BIRDS

Subtle in his strangeness,
he knew about narrative,
and he knew about the dark.

His birds begin as shadows,
intimations of the unknown.
The silence is tangible.
Then the staccato sound.
When nature takes vengeance
there is no more melody.

The fat man's secret:
we wish, we fear, we love
while the birds wait.
They are our end.

Hitchcock takes flight.

LA BELLE ET LA BETE

Her innocence he found enveloping:
he did not want her revealed
as another naked woman
for the world to see.
Beauty was to be his private pleasure,

In silken adornment
her presence invited him,
more than the fruit itself
that he could take at any time,
devour, and so be alone again.

He woke from dreams in disappointment,
for love had made him imagine
that he might sleep again,
and make of him another.

In his nights she was high born,
an African princess
adorned in ivory
cool against her charcoal skin.
Her dreams were of hunters
with weathered faces before the fire
in forest depths where cascading water
flowed in perpetual torrent.
Every shadow was a stranger
to be stilled by sweet sounds.
He called out her name
in the wild, entangled in thorns.

Something was seeking him.
One word alone was spoken.

When the silence was broken
in the clear light of morning
the door of her chamber opened
at the gasp she gave of love.

SOMETIMES IN THE ROMAN NIGHT

She stands by the window,
aware of herself in the evening air.
Views from her high vantage
always impress at first glance,
and even now enrich her.
Sunset winds sweep the valley floor,
rippling the river patterns,
worrying the trees in the piazza.
She will wear silk tonight,
an occasion for umbrellas,
and a hurrying from taxis.

Revellers grow weary of themselves,
exhausted by excess.
Pleasure palls in wild seasons.
But they are not where she is now,
screened behind colonnades,
drinking deeply an admirer's wine
into the single chime of morning.

There will be another day
to remember her elegance.
Memory is of might-have-beens.
Perhaps for her a finer thought:
sometimes the air is surprised by storms.

HERMIONE THE HUMMINGBIRD'S DREAM

Was it the Mayflower she sailed
when we heard an unfamiliar call?
Hermione's song was innocent no more,
having tasted the waters,
and in the heartbreak spellbound.
The chain is broken -
all is absent thought of her -
the door of the cage has opened.
The human hummingbird
to the delight of all has flown.
Hermione sings of the freedom
nowhere to be seen
but in her dream,
the feather-winged woman
she believes herself to be.
Making her way in the universe,
now the wild-minded heroine
spinning over oceans.
Hermione on the horizon,
rising as a star.

ANOTHER TIME, ANOTHER SONG

We sing our lives in a fragile world,
learning the words that will survive us.
They rise as easily as the sun
when the dawn hour arrives,
and for a moment the rhythm is stilled.
Dare we imagine another time?

These thoughts fly over the moon.
We see ourselves out there,
being only who we are.
The song we sing is from a distant life
older than any memory we hear.
Ever the same song in with different sound.

WHEN I FELL

When I fell for her we began to travel.
Life became a pattern of departures
to read of Icarus and to reach the sun.

Sharing our world is a way of writing
postcards to the past, each one saying Yes
that sets the world inflight.

My bride adorned rests
with eyes of many cities.
There are continents to cross,
We open those hidden doors
where the waters are timelessly flowing.
Age-old oxen plough in dreamtime.
The air itself is music.

When I fell for her there was no motion to compare.
The earth was weightless, the moon a madman's lantern.
Every thought a perfect word.
She shakes her hair, and a diamond falls.
The leaves of spring attend her.
Summer lingers into a temperate time.
Consider how the seasons become her.

UNE PENSEE SIMPLE

Tu est toujours toi-même,
une porte ouverte,
une fenêtre fermée.
Elles sont la présence
dans mon cœur.
Tu es mon cœur.

Il y a une foule dehors,
mais ici personne
parce que je suis rien
sans ton sourire
dans l'aube
dans la nuit.

A crowd gathers, though there is no-one
because I am nothing without your smile
in the night and at dawn.

Always yourself.
A door opens, a window closes.
They are there in my heart.
You are my heart.

www.ingramcontent.com/pod-product-compliance
Lightning Source LLC
LaVergne TN
LVHW041238150826
845673LV00008B/2425

* 9 7 8 8 1 1 9 2 2 8 1 8 8 *